THE FISHERMAN'S WORLD
IN PICTURES

THE FISHERMAN'S WORLD
IN PICTURES

Sláva Štochl

Hamlyn

Translated by Helga Hanks
Designed and produced by ARTIA for
THE HAMLYN PUBLISHING GROUP LIMITED
London • New York • Sydney • Toronto
Hamlyn House, Feltham, Middlesex, England

ISBN 0 600 01332 4

Printed in Czechoslovakia

CONTENTS

Today only a few white spaces are left on the map. Driven by the inexorable urge to explore, man has filled in one after the other, has conquered what used to be thought unconquerable. He has climbed the highest mountain peaks, has penetrated the jungle and crossed endless deserts. He has descended into the deepest abysses and has overcome the gravitational pull of the earth, voyaging into space. And yet there still exists on this earth a world into which we cannot see — the world of the waters. Today almost every aspect of life beneath the glassy surface of the water has been explored, most of the living creatures are named, but the mystery of it remains. The depths of the waters still have power to fascinate us, there are still surprises, and only reluctantly does the water yield her secrets to the eyes of man.

Water — rivers, brooks or the great expanses of lakes — is a source of continual change, fascinating the mind of man. Just sit down sometime on the bank and cast your eye over the water. You will be surprised how many different pictures you will see. Here the water is clear and transparent, here it runs turbulently, and there again stormy waves dash on the shore. And if you just once take hold of a rod, you are lost for ever. You are left alone with your river, and in your mind there is no room for the everyday things, the stream has swept all away with a new, stronger experience. You are calm and yet filled with the passionate excitement of the hunt. Patiently you sit by the water's edge, waiting tensely for the moment when the calm changes into action, and the stillness is shattered by a dramatic duel. Will it be a big one or a small one that is hooked and with one tremendous leap comes flying across the water, or goes fleeing into the depths? But the water is silent, and its seemingly endless peacefulness becomes almost a part of your being. You feel yourself becoming part of Nature. You walk over pebbles which the stream has shaped and smoothed for hundreds of years; you seek out those places where the fish have had their habitation since human memory began. Your frail rod binds you to the very life of the waters.

The angler who comes to the water for the first time has one idea and only one idea in his head, and that is to catch a fish. This is why he has started out with his fishing gear in the first place. He is determined to find his fish, to make it take his bait and, by some method, get it out of the water. The river is for him only the means to an end, and he expects nothing more from it. He sets out before dawn, overcoming all obstacles to reach his prey. He is impatient, and a restless hunting instinct drives him from one place to another. But as water and time flow past him, unbeknown to him, a great change comes over the angler. He still has his hunting instinct, but it is no longer just the prey that draws him to the river. He is calmer now he has conquered the fish, he delights in his catch, but in a different way. He is filled with admiration for the fish and the milieu in which he has caught it. He becomes aware of the surroundings of the river, the flowers on the bank, and from time to time puts down his rod and looks around him, enjoying the beauty which somehow he has never noticed before. His attitude to the fish is a different one, too. Earlier, the fish was no more than his prey — the bigger the better — but today he sees the fish as a living creature, not necessarily only there to be caught.

For the beginner the rod is only a means of securing the fish. Fearing to loose it, he chooses the strongest rod and the strongest hook. Only once he has realized that he can master the fish with sensitivity and complete familiarity, by using the finer points of angling technique, does the transformation take place from mere hunter to true sporstman, and at the same time he becomes a lover of nature.

A man who has fallen, heart and soul, in love with the sport of angling and can hardly conceive existence without those frequent excursions to the water, can indulge his passion almost the whole year round. In spring wild mountain streams await him. It is an exacting pursuit over difficult terrain, scrambling along almost impassable banks, and contending with torrents in full flood, but the reward for all this exertion lies in fat trout and Char. In the slower streams of the foothills the Grayling are bewitching in their sublimity, while it is an exhilarating experience for the angler to go after the Danubian Salmon, the king of the mountain streams and river rapids. In still lakes the angler will find Char and Rainbow Trout, and in the waters of low-lying plains, Pike, large Catfish, Pike-perch, Eels, and other predatory fish, as well as Carp, Tench, and many other fish, large and small, common and rare. He can go river-fishing any time from spring to winter, even in ice and snow — as long as he can stand cold and frost!

We are anglers — millions of anglers throughout the world. We fish in fresh water and sea water, and our love of the sport must be passionate indeed, for it drags us from the comfort of our warm homes out into all kinds of weather. We are driven perhaps by something which the generality of mankind has lost centuries ago — a longing for Nature in its purest state, with our longing for the river. At the water's side we are quite different people — more peaceful, more at ease, and perhaps also more happy. The purity of Nature makes its impression on us, and we are ready to make friends with others who have the same interests as ourselves. But friendship on the riverbank is rare, uncertain, and easily destroyed. During the actual angling it is exposed to many hazards, but if it can surmount selfishness, envy, and pettiness, it can grow into a fine and lasting thing. The man who can take pleasure in your catch as much as his own, who will take you to his favourite spots where good fish are to be caught, is a true friend. The joy in a good day's sport is a double joy, and every setback is only half as bad.

But there exists another king of friendship, very common among anglers, even though it is generally not very widely recognized — friendship with things. Few sportsmen treasure their equipment as much as anglers do. They pamper and look after their rods with a positively touching affection, and they talk about them as if they were creatures. They take a delight in their characters, their shape, their construction, and if they are forced to be parted from their rods, it is like taking leave of a real friend. Old or broken rods, which can be used no more, stay in the house, for they have done good service. On innumerable occasions they have been guides, protectors, and helpers, and have grown to be a part of the angler's own life. The landing nets and fishing baskets in which the best catches of his life have lain, are kept in service for as long as possible, and are repaired again and again. And a similar care is expended on the line, the reel, and everything else which accompanies the angler on his trips to the water.

A friendship with Nature is struck up which lasts one's whole life. Again and again we journey back to her, again and again we do battle along the banks of the rivers, and dream of the catch of our life, the golden fish which will enable us to fulfil our greatest wish : to be able to sit for ever more at the water's edge and renew our happiness in the lap of Nature again and again for ever.

THE WORLD OF THE MOUNTAIN STREAM

The life of the river begins high in the mountains. Mist,
rain, and melting snowfields feed tiny streams which flow
down towards the valleys, leaping merrily over rocks and
boulders. This is the kingdom of the Brown Trout. Hungry
almost all the year round, the Brown Trout withstands,
hidden behind a boulder, the force of the rushing water —
and the melting masses of snow. No, it is not an easy
life, but the trout does not leave its inhospitable but
clean and pure mountain stream. It is the first
member of the salmon family, preferring all kinds of
turbulent waters, from tiny mountain streams to the
rushing torrents of the foothills. Wherever clean
water, rich in oxygen, presents favourable conditions
for them, we find the salmon family, and are amazed by
the beauty of their bodies, their wonderful colours and
their strong will, asserting themselves in a world of purity
and movement

Alone, lost in the solitude
of the mountains, the angler experiences
minutes full of tension
and excitement

In rough currents and in quiet pools
lie hidden those secrets which it is
the angler's longing to uncover.
Cautiously, he moves upstream,
searching the water with his eyes.
For a brief moment the bait dances
on the ripples of the surface,
then it sinks calmly and slowly
into the green depths

above, a stony and gravelly river-bed,
from which it is hard to distinguish
the Brown Trout *(Salmo trutta var. fario)* which
lies motionless in the current,
waiting to pounce like lightning on any victim
which may come its way,
whether from the air or through the water

Every angler knows the song of the rapids.
In the springtime when the rivers are filled
with melt-water, it is a tempestuous symphony,
later becoming tender and calm.
This song is the constant accompaniment
of the angler as he wades through the stream,
his eyes fixed on the bait dancing on the water

Trout are the jewels of the mountain and hill streams,
jewels which it is the angler's aim to win
at any price. Neither the roughest currents nor
the thickest undergrowth along the river bank will deter him.
He jumps from boulder to boulder, balancing
on loose and slippery stones in the water,
all for the sake of the unforgettable moment
when he casts his fly at the right place
beneath the waterfall and a golden form,
flecked with red, appears from the water
and snatches at the hook

mountain lakes and reservoirs,
ere conditions are particularly favourable
its development, the trout
ches record size. Here we find old and wary fish, weighing up
eleven pounds. To get such a monster on one's rod
match one's skill against its is
unforgettable experience for any angler

The Brown Trout is a predator, and every catch
a joy for an experienced and dedicated angler.
Every real sportsman prefers the fly-rod technique
to any other type of fishing.
Only in places where we can expect really large trout,
which can seldom be caught with a fly,
will we use the spinner with spoonbait
or with some other artificial bait

A glorious moment
in the life of the angler:
after a dramatic fight
the shining body
of a huge trout
is lying in the
landing net

Apparently inauspicious brooks running
through the meadows may have quite
a number of surprises in store
for the angler. Here too he may
well find quite a large trout
suddenly darting out of its hiding place
underneath the overhanging bank
of the stream. It is entirely
a matter of the angler's skill
whether he can catch the trout
or whether he is left disappointed,
seeing the fish race away

Only if one is particularly skilful
in casting the fly will one be able
to try one's luck on a river
overgrown with thick weeds or reeds

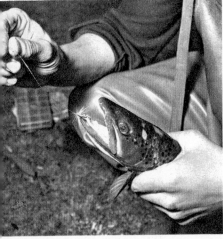

The Brown Trout is a fish of prey,
and its attack on the bait is wild
and passionate. If the bait looks too
artificial or is not cast properly
the fish will become suspicious
and will not take the bait

The angler has to concentrate on every cast
and then wait in straining suspense
for the moment when the fish attacks.
At last it happens. But the man on the river bank
does not know whether it is another
trout or some other member of the salmon family,
whose shining body can soon be seen
breaking the surface of the water

When insects are circling low over a trout-brook,
we can observe the graceful leaps of the trout.
As long as the fish hunt insects swimming on the water,
we can only observe a ripple and movement on the water's
surface. But if the trout start to catch insects flying
above the water's surface they have to leap clear
of the water in a fine arc. Rainbow Trout
are particularly fine leapers

Catching a Rainbow Trout with an artificial fly
is a marvellous experience for any angler.
The fine, light tackle used for fly fishing makes
it possible for the trout to fight for a long time.
It performs heroic leaps, landing with a splash
on the surface of the water, and plunges down
to the bottom, where it writhes to be
free of the hook

The Rainbow Trout of rivers and moving water
has a body-structure similar to that of the
Brown Trout. In still waters, reservoirs,
and lakes, where it does not have to fight against
the current and where it can find sufficient
nourishment, it becomes more compact and larger.
Here the angler needs stronger tackle
and a large spoon-bait, for there is always
the chance of coming across a really splendid
specimen. The fight with a big Rainbow Trout
is quite a duel. The fish constantly changes
its tactics. It races along on the bottom,
only to leap clean out of the water a moment later

The big Rainbow Trout caught in deep waters
is a veritable water tiger.
It is no easy matter to induce it
to attack the fly. But the joy of the angler
is so much the greater at catching such
a splendid specimen

Minutes of tension and concentration.
We have cast our line in unknown waters
beneath a weir. The spoon-bait is swimming
in the current, over shallow and deep waters,
here sparkling next to a stone,
there between the roots of a tree.
At any moment we expect a fish to attack,
to see the shining body in the water and
the excitement of the pull on the rod

The magic that lures
us back to the river
every time is simple:
the sun, water
and the fish
in clear currents

Every brook, every deep pool in the water
has its secrets which are not revealed
to the eyes of inquisitive mankind

Only the fishing rod can bring those secrets
to the surface. But skill and technique
are necessary to persuade the fish to bite,
and to land it safely

What seemed to us to be shadows and roots
suddenly come to life and follow curiously
this facinating, shimmering thing whirling
in the water. The spoon-bait fascinates and repels
the fish at the same time. Above all, though,
it provokes them to attack — which most
of them pay for with their life

The Brook Trout *(Salvelinus fontinalis)*, which we find
in clean, fast-flowing mountain rivers, also belongs
to the salmon family. It too is a fish of prey,
which attacks the bait viciously and is able
to fight obstinately

The Brook Trout is caught either with spoon-bait
or artificial fly. Like all the other fish
of prey the Brook Trout lies in wait for its victims
under embankments or among tree roots.
As soon as it sees a suitable prey,
it rushes forward out of the dark into the
clear water, and returns again to
its former hiding place

The Brook Trout is a hardy and modest fish.
As far as oxygen is concerned it
is not as demanding as the trout,
and also is capable of living in very cold spring water,
where other fish cannot survive

We can follow with our eyes the Brook Trout's attack
if we fish in a clear mountain lake.
It appears like lightning from its hiding place,
and snatches the bait

he battle with a Brook Trout can become very dramatic,
articularly when it is with a large specimen.
'he fish will fight on for a long time,
ith great patience, and surrender only
hen it is totally exhausted.
s size depends, as with the Brown Trout,
n its surroundings. Usually in small brooks,
nly small Brook Trout are to be found.
n larger waters, where the fish has
lenty of scope for food,
e can catch Brook Trout weighing several pounds

If we look carefully into the clear, quiet mountain rivers, we can see
the long shadows of fishes. Different from the trout in shape,
and found in places where no trout would venture, these are
Graylings, the beauties of slow-moving streams

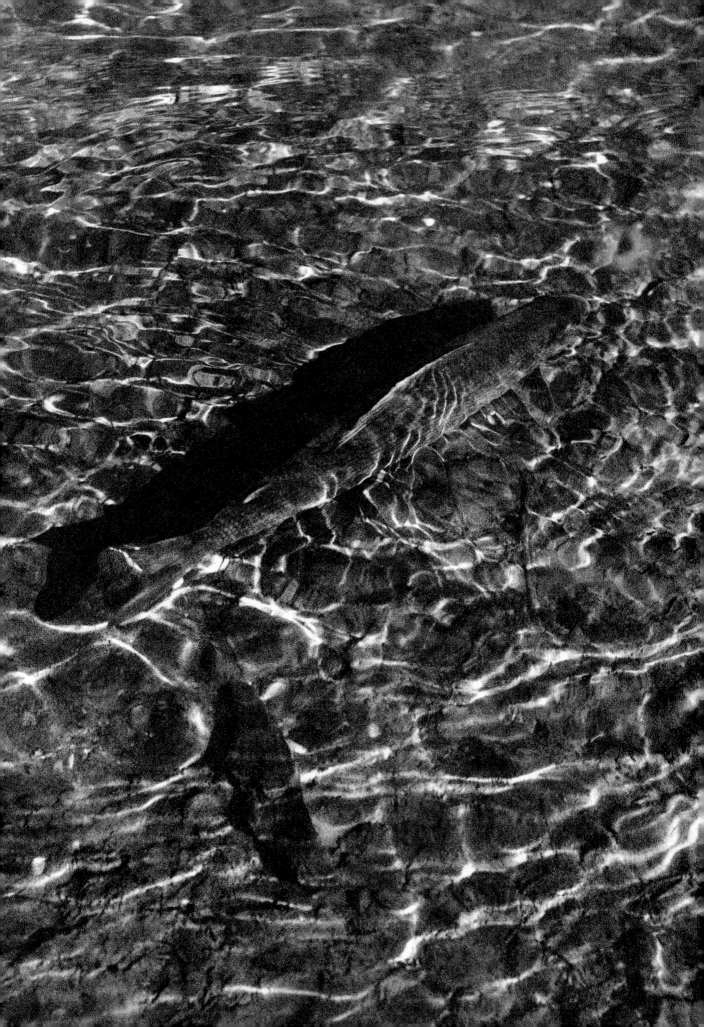

It is possible to distinguish the Grayling *(Thymallus thymallus)* at first sight from the other members of the salmon family, mainly because of the perfect streamlining of the sides of its flat body. Depending upon the time of day, the light conditions, and the weather, Grayling may be found alternating between motionless parts of the water and out in the main currents. Unlike the trout and Char, they do not hide under overhanging banks, but stay at the bottom of the river, where they lie in wait, watching the currents

The Grayling is a particularly mistrustful,
moody, and choosy fish, feeding mainly on water
and air insects. It is caught with flies, which
we either swim on the water or which we let 'drown'.
The catching of a Grayling demands a lot of skill
and sensitivity, because we can only use delicate tackle
and the smallest artificial flies. The Grayling
with its mistrustful eye will notice the smallest inaccuracy,
and if our fly does not look like a real insect
the fish will not bite

When the Grayling chases insects swimming on the water,
all that we can see is a series of little ripples
on the surface. This is the moment which the angler
has to wait for. He must, with a skilful cast,
place the artificial fly just in line with the place
where the Grayling is hunting. If the fly does not
look suspicious to the Grayling it will bite.
Now starts the fight: either the Grayling ends up
in the landing net or it will tear itself free
of the delicate hook, in which case the angler
has no choice but to try his luck once again

The Grayling is a beautiful fish,
even if it cannot boast the same rich colouring
as the trout or Char. It is coloured grey-green
to blue, with a shimmer of mother-of-pearl.
Its most beautiful ornament is the dorsal fin,
a high, long flag — particularly in the male — with
a black chequerboard pattern on a purple base

The best time for catching Grayling is in the autumn.
The water is colder and as there are not
so many insects left, the Grayling feels the need
for food. Even the large Graylings, who looked at our bait
in the summer with contempt, are now easier to outwit

The Sea Trout *(Salmo trutta)*
is a somewhat rarer fish of the
larger mountain streams.
It prefers strong currents.
The Sea Trout is a migratory fish,
which following the dictates of Nature,
leaves the North Sea and journeys up
to the upper tributaries of
European rivers to spawn

Was it playfulness or curiosity which made the Sea Trout,
enchanted by the unknown shining and whirling thing
in the water, emerge beside the bait?
It showed itself a couple of times to the surprised
angler — but did not bite. All his efforts were without
success, the change of bait quite useless. The Sea Trout
saw through his tricks, and had disappeared, not to be
seen again

An exhilarating battle takes place in the torrents
of a mountain river. In the deeper parts of the river,
where on the border between the torrent and the eddy,
a Sea Trout seizes the spoon. After the catch
it writhes around on the surface of the water, showing
itself in all its beauty, and a moment later flees upstream.
One dramatic moment follows another.
The fish fights in every possible position. It lets the current
carry it and descends to the bottom to gain new strength.
At last its resistance breaks, and the happy angler
is able to bring the catch to the surface

The vanquished Sea Trout shines silver,
and we can admire the beauty of its body,
completely adapted as it is to contending with
raging torrents. Nature has equipped
the fish well for coping with the strength
of such currents and for covering
the huge distances which it has to travel
on its way to the spawning grounds

Another large fish of European rivers is the Danubian
Salmon *(Hucho hucho)*. While the Sea Trout is an
inhabitant of the rivers flowing into the North Sea,
the Danubian Salmon belongs to the Danube and its
tributaries. Long ago it used to move into the smaller
rivers flowing into the Danube to spawn.
Pollution of the tributaries and the erection
of insurmountable obstacles such as dams, have made
migration impossible for Danubian Salmon, and so
they have become permanent inhabitants
of deeper rivers and reservoirs

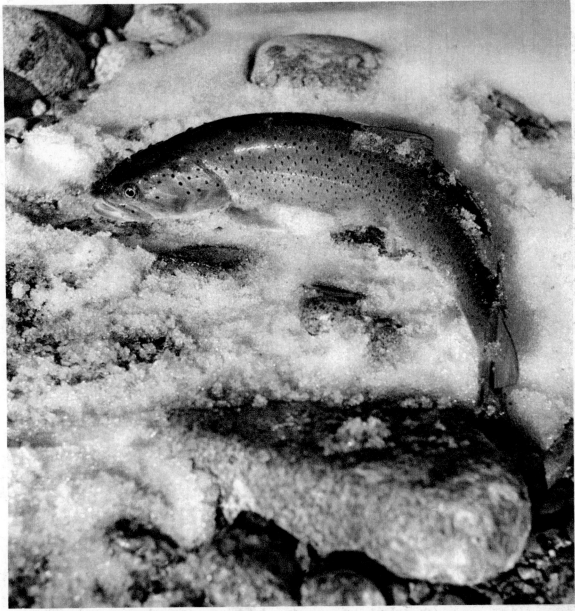

Clear water becomes treacherous for the fish.
The large blurred shadows which we can see
at the bottom are Danubian Salmon.
The middle-sized fish live in shoals on the
bottom whereas larger specimens live singly
in the deep waters and rapids,
where they hide under stones,
lying in wait for their prey

The Danubian Salmon attacks its prey
suddenly and wildly. It rushes out
of its hiding place, chasing just below
the surface the smaller fishes,
which try to escape the reach of the
terrible teeth by leaping out of the water

It is a peculiar feeling to fish in a river
where we know that large Danubian Salmon
are to be found. Strict concentration is necessary here.
With every cast the angler must expect the attack
of a huge predatory fish. At every bite he expects
that strong pull which means that he has got
a large Danubian Salmon on his rod.
The Danubian Salmon bites at all levels in the water —
in the depths where it remains unseen until landed,
as well as on the surface where we can follow its wild leaps

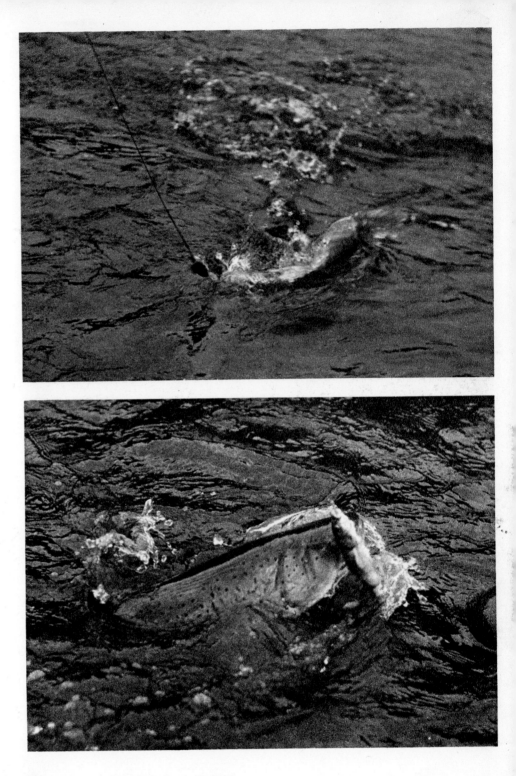

Following a trolled bait (a small fish),
appears the shining back of a large fish,
and the angler feels a rough tug on the rod.
Immediately he strikes, and the fish is hooked

It has been a long
and hard struggle, for
the Danubian Salmon
fights wildly
and obstinately.
But at last it loses
its strength
and is pulled to the
shallow water
and then lifted out

The main season for catching Danubian Salmon
starts in the winter. The smaller fish
retreat to their winter quarters.
The Danubian Salmon begins to suffer
from the lack of food and so throws itself
greedily on to the bait. It is at this time
that the biggest specimens are caught, which could
not be persuaded to bite in the autumn

The catch lies in the snow

The catching of Danubian Salmon in winter is
a strenuous and hard sport.
During a hard frost there are ice-floes in the river;
the line freezes in the ice, and ice jams the reel.
But the enthusiastic angler cannot be kept away from
the river even by the most inclement weather.
And if at this moment out there in the river
a Danubian Salmon takes the bait all one's
troubles are forgotten. With the catching of a Danubian
Salmon in the depths of winter we say goodbye to the
salmon family of the mountain brooks, rivers, and lakes

N CALM, DEEP WATERS

The rivers have left the mountain region and have become calmer and wider. They no longer rush over roots and stones, they are deep and mysterious; the water is warmer and richer in food.

Here many species of fish may be found, with widely different characteristics. Most of them feed on small creatures living in the water, and on water plants. We call them non-predatory fish in contrast to the fish of prey which hunt smaller fishes and any other animal living in the water.

The peaceful waters of the lowlands also have their charms for the angler, even if it is a very different charm from that of the wild mountain streams. Here he looks for peace and relaxation as he sits by the water beside his rod. But it is not always as quiet as this. If the angler casts his bait to catch a fish of prey he may experience quite a dramatic fight. It is entirely up to the angler to choose the form of angling which suits him best.

The river flows along, apparently peaceful and sublime.
And yet countless dramatic episodes take place
in its impenetrable depths. Only occasionally
does the river show its real face. The surface of the water
begins to ripple, and we can observe small fishes leaping
and fleeing helplessly in confusion from the big predatory
fish which is hunting them

In the dark depths of the river, under the shadow
of the bank or at the edge of the reeds,
lies the Pike *(Esox lucius)*, apparently motionless
and passive. Only an almost imperceptible movement
of its fins tells one that its passivity
is no more than a disguise of its real character.
As soon as an innocent fish comes within reach
of its vicious teeth, the Pike rushes forward
and seizes the prey.

At a Pike pool

The Pike has taken
the live bait,
a small fish.
All is still quiet.
The Pike is either
eating the bait or
swimming along
near the bottom,
the bait in its mouth.
Only when the angler
tightens the line
and the fish feels
the resistance of the
line does the battle
begin

To start off with
the Pike tries to get
rid of the hook by force.
If this is unsuccessful
it will try to loosen
the hook by leaping
across the water,
shaking its open mouth

The prey caught by the Pike has no chance.
It crushes the prey with the powerful back
teeth of its lower jaw; and the countless
inward-curved teeth of its upper jaw
make it impossible for the prey to escape

The angler has cast the line
at a well-known Pike haunt.
Suddenly the fish dives.
Only the spinning reel shows
that the Pike is swimming towards
the middle of the river,
carrying the bait.
There the fish pauses for a moment
and the angler strikes immediately.
The line cuts the surface of the water
and the fish swims swiftly along
very close to the bottom.
Not once does it show itself above
the water, and a steady pull
on the line is the only sign
of its presence. Having reached
the further bank the fish tries
to entangle the line in the reeds
but at long last is forced
to surrender, and the angler can lift
the Pike out of the water
with his landing net

To catch a large Pike, to battle it into
exhaustion and finally to conquer it —
that is a dream which can become a reality
for many an angler. There are still plenty
of waters inhabited by splendid,
record-breaking specimens; large reservoirs,
brooks that can never be exhausted of their
supply of fish, and the quiet tributaries
of larger rivers. Every year catches
of well over thirty pounds are recorded. The lucky
one who comes across such a catch,
will tell the most incredible stories
about the battle with 'his' Pike.
The three Pikes in our picture were caught
in the calmer tributaries of the Danube

The autumn is the most beautiful season,
and also the most suitable time of year
to catch Pike, because then fishing with a spoon
and other artificial bait begins.
Spinning is a very popular type of fishing,
because quite a lot of skill is needed to find the Pike
and then persuade it to take the bait

The spoon cast into the water will sink slowly.
And then it starts rotating slowly and
moving backwards, drawn in by the reel.
Even in the murky depth the fish notices the shining
metal spoon. The Pike has a special organ,
called the lateral line, which makes it possible for it,
even before it has seen the bait,
to notice the movement of the water, and it
attacks swift as an arrow

The Pike usually takes the bait at a considerable depth;
the angler therefore only notices the strong pull
on the tackle, to which he must react immediately.
The next fraction of a second is perhaps the most
marvellous moment of spinning. We wait to see what will
happen. A strong pull means that a fish is hooked;
if the line remains still it means that the bait has got
caught up in some obstruction in the water

A successful catch,
in the light
of an autumn sunset

The quiet pool becomes a battleground, if we come
across a Pike in the peaceful water. With a terrific flick
of its tail the fish leaps out of the water
and flies through the air, trying to shake off the hook
by opening its mouth wide. It repeats this leap a couple
of times, and if the angler is not skilful enough,
and the hook does not hold tight enough, the fish
gains its freedom easily. The reason the Pike
leaps above the surface of the water is that
the water's resistance does not allow it
to move as swiftly as it can in the air

There is no need for the angler to put his fishing tackle
into store in the winter.
On the solidly frozen surface of the water of a reservoir
the angler can wait for his catch beside
a hole picked in the ice. As bait for fishing in the
ice small fishes or spinners are most useful.
The ground-bait is allowed to sink to the bottom,
and then the artificial bait is alternately let down
and pulled to the surface of the water

The best success can be expected
at noon on a sunny winter's day.
By lifting the bait the angler
feels that a fish is hooked
and immediately after the strike
the battle with the unknown adversary
concealed beneath the ice, begins.
The Pike is not quite so aggressive
in the winter and therefore
even large specimens are comparatively easy
to vanquish and pull on top of the ice

We can of course capture a number of other fish
in the rivers of the lowlands. One of them
is the Pike-perch *(Stizostedion lucioperca)*.
This representative of the perch family can in isolated cases
reach a weight of over twenty pounds. It is no less
a predator than the Pike, living in shoals and preferring
those parts of the river with alternating light currents
and deeper pools, running over stony or sandy ground.
During the last few years the Pike-perch,
originally an inhabitant of deep lakes,
has found excellent living conditions in deep reservoirs

We can catch the Pike-perch by various methods,
either with a bait of dead fish or
with spinners, which are either trolled from
the river bank or from a boat.
With small spinners, which are trolled
through the depth, we can feel the fish bite.
We can determine immediately from the
movement of the water and the behaviour of the line
that it is not a Pike, and when a silvery
shining body appears on the surface
we know that our assumption has been correct.
It is a large Pike-perch that is
fighting with the tackle

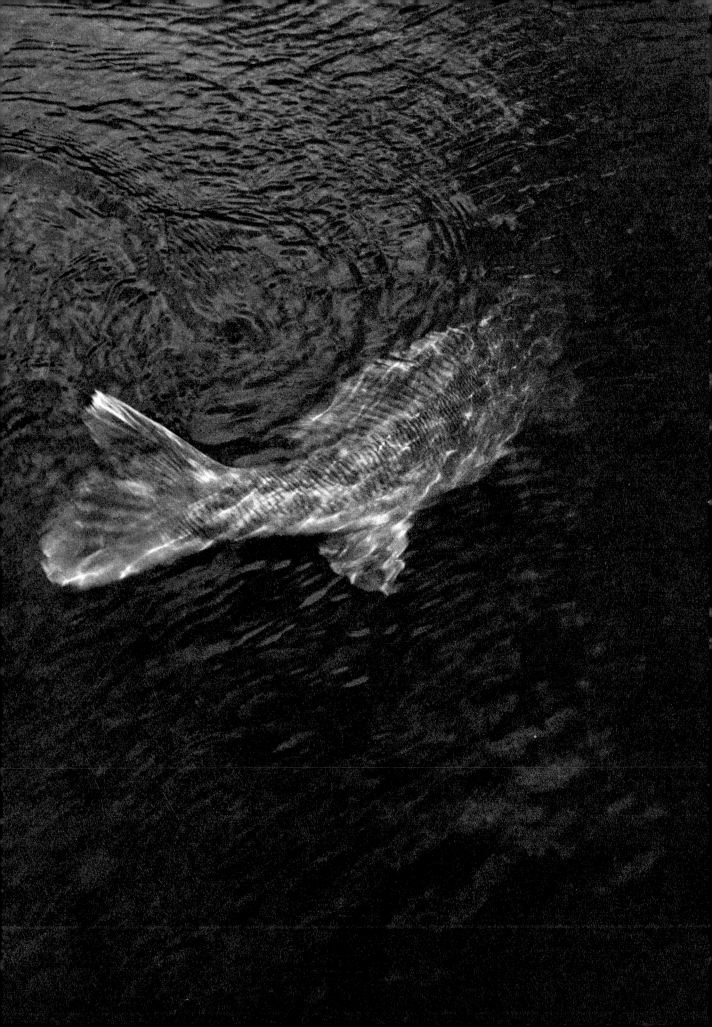

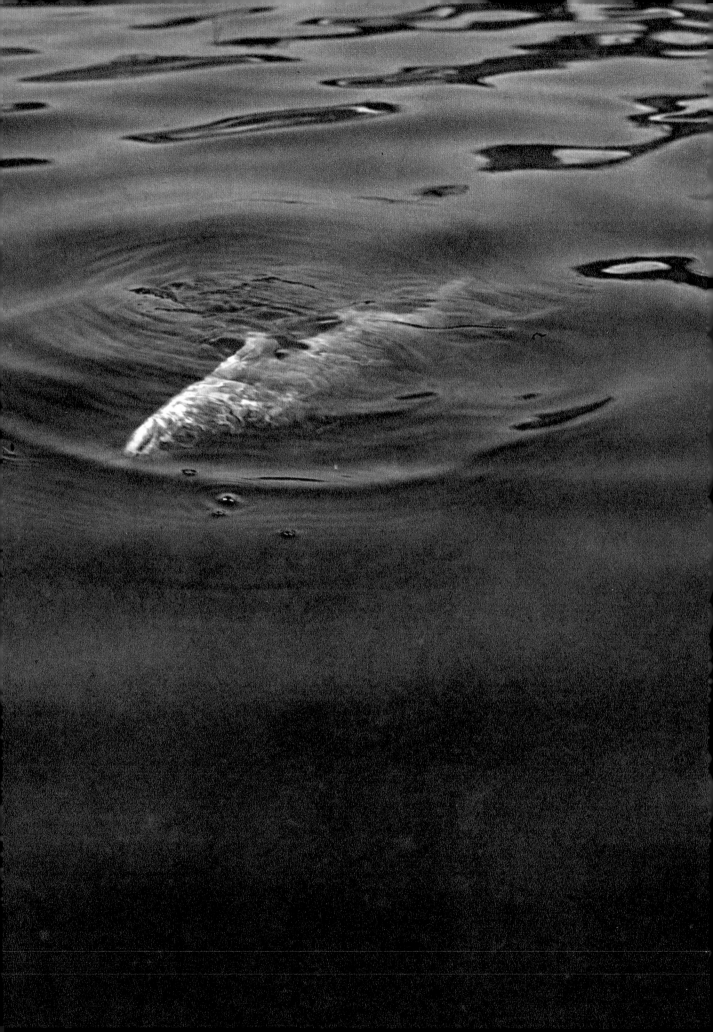

As the angler may not expect violent leaps
and surprise escaping tactics, the battle
with the Pike-perch is not all that exciting. The Pike-perch
will try to escape, but gives in very soon

Though it is not difficult to overpower the Pike-perch
once it is hooked, it is extremely difficult to provoke
it to bite. It is moody and mistrustful, and one of the most
unpredictable fishes known. Sometimes one cannot hook a single
Pike-perch for a long time in places where there are
many present, and then in another part of the river they bite wildly,
snapping the bait from under one another's noses.
But this unpredictability and uncertainty is the special
attraction of fishing for Pike-perch, and every large
Pike-perch caught makes the angler's heart beat faster

The Catfish *(Silurus glanis)* lives in deep and peaceful
slow-moving rivers and reservoirs, and is the largest fish
of prey in fresh water. It prefers deep potholes with slowly
flowing waters and the bottom overgrown with weeds

Spinning on a river
with large areas
of weeds and roots,
the most popular
location of the Catfish

The Catfish is, as might be expected on account of its size,
an extremely persevering fighter, which quite often will put up a fight
against its captor lasting several hours. A large Catfish determines
the rules of the battle itself. It swims with the current
wherever it likes, goes right down to the bottom
where it suits it, and the angler must try, come what may,
to keep the fish away from places where he could entangle the line
and tear it. It is an exhausting fight, and the end is often uncertain.
Nevertheless, many an angler has achieved a fine catch of Catfish,
and there are records of catches weighing between 100 and 170 pounds

The Catfish usually bites in the deep parts of the water,
and therefore we only notice that one is hooked on our
tackle when we feel the strong resistance after the bite.
Only rarely does the Catfish hunt on the surface of the
water, and it is then that the surprised angler
sees in the rippling water a dark, wedge-shaped body
come up and dive away again

In former days the Catfish was a comparatively rare catch.
The fishing tackle then in use was totally inadequate for catching
a heavy and strong fish like this. It was not strong enough
and a large Catfish could get rid of the hook very easily by tearing
the line or breaking the rod. Only modern techniques of
fishing and modern equipment, light rods, strong lines,
and efficient reels have made it possible for the angler to
provoke this fish to attack the spinner
and after a long struggle land it successfully

Only now is it possible to see how rich
the waters of the lowlands are in Catfish,
and that it is possible to overpower
a large fish by applying skill and strength

The large reservoirs provide the Catfish
with very favourable living conditions.
Large expanses of water, plentiful food,
and the warm water found at the edge of the reservoir
and on the surface are the conditions favourable
to the quick growth of the Catfish, which,
particularly in reservoirs, reach enormous weights
and are numbered among the largest fish
that we can catch in fresh waters

The body of the Catfish reminds one of an enormous
tadpole. The powerful flat head with its wide mouth has
frightened many a novice. It is therefore not very
surprising that people in the past should have seen the
powerful, slippery body of the Catfish with its long barbels
hunting at the surface of the water, and made out of
it in their imagination a supernatural being,
a water sprite, living in underwater caverns

The angler hauls the Catfish out
of the water using an ice hook.
Smaller specimens are seized
by their lower jaw

Before winter sets in the Catfish retreats
to calm and deep parts of the water,
where it finds its winter quarters in a deep hollow.
During this time it takes very little food
and may easily fall prey to a pike-angler

It is really something of a wonder
that in the deep parts of our lowland rivers
there are still today such large fish.
If the angler is lucky he will manage
to catch one of these monsters

The murky depths, the continuing hope
of a splendid specimen —
all this lures the angler to the river
over and over again

That mysterious rover of the waters,
the Eel *(Anguilla anguilla)* is one of the
most interesting of fish which live —
as the Eel does for at least a part of its life —
in fresh water

The Eel hunts at night and most frequently during twilight.
When the sun disappears beneath the horizon
the nightly battle for survival begins in the water,
and the angler waits for the Eels to start biting

he Eel and its way of life has been the subject
f many bold guesses and hypotheses,
nd it took many years of research before
nything positive was known about its life
1 fresh water and sea water. But even today
is still a mysterious and legendary
1habitant of the waters

A thunderstorm is approaching over the river. This is the
best time to catch Eels. A fish is biting at the bait which
we throw on to the surface of the water in the light
of the approaching thunderstorm

The long snake-like body is struggling
against the tackle, and tries to escape
into the depths of the water. But even
when the fish has been overpowered and has
been pulled out of the water
in the landing-net it still continues
to struggle, and will not give up trying
to escape back into the water

The Eel differs from other fish not only in the shape
of its body but also because of its living habits.
It is a predatory fish, which hides in murky water
during the day, and appears only towards the evening
to do its hunting. It lives in lowland
and mountain rivers, and travels thousands of miles
during its lifetime. The Eel spawns near the Bahamas
and in the Sargasso Sea, and the spawn are carried
to the coast of Europe by the Gulf Stream.
The larvae develop into young Eels —
called elvers — in the river-mouths of Europe.
The elvers ascend the rivers and remain there for
several years. During this time they grow fairly rapidly
and are often called yellow Eels. The Eels return
between the ages of six and twenty from the rivers to
the sea. Why some of them undertake this migration
comparatively early, while others grow to a weight
of up to eleven pounds, remains a mystery.
Nevertheless, these large, predatory, and aggressive
fish remain a cherished prey for the angler

Another nocturnal predator, which prefers especially
the clear, wild waters inhabited by trout, is the Burbot
(*Lota lota*). It is the terror of trout, and known as a
predator of spawn and fry. The Burbot is an insatiable
creature and does not even spare its own kind, devouring
everything that comes within reach

An unwanted predator of trout brooks,
the Burbot is a much sought-after prey for anglers
in the reservoirs of the lowlands. They are caught
in the winter months, angled for through ice,
and always shortly before nightfall

we use a spinner or other animal bait to catch predatory
h, the Perch *(Perca fluviatilis)* will be the most likely
ch. It is found everywhere in brooks, rivers, pools,
d lakes, from the lowlands and coastal plains to the
ut streams of the mountains

Smaller Perch can bring anglers to despair,
for they snap up the bait or pull at it, preventing
a bigger catch. A large Perch however, is a very
welcome catch. In larger rivers and in reservoirs
Perch will be found weighing up to seven pounds,
and in view of their aggressiveness, their pugnaciousness,
and their excellent taste, they are a very popular catch

Another fish of prey living in the waters of the lowlands is the Asp *(Aspius aspius)*, which is found in clean, large rivers, where it moves alternately from the stronger currents and quiet parts. It has a voracious appetite, not hesitating to swallow a fly, or a small fish, which it will chase along the surface, making a great disturbance

The Asp is a most intelligent fish and is not easy to outwit. It may be caught with live bait or artificial bait, like all predatory fish. The most enjoyable and sporting method is using the fly rod with a large fly. The Asp can weigh up to eleven pounds and a duel with such a fish is quite an experience

In shallow backwaters, light currents and still waters,
shoals of silver shining fishes can be observed swimming
slowly forwards and backwards. These are the Chub
(*Leuciscus cephalus*), and they belong to the carp family.
They are omnivorous, and vegetable or animal
bait can be used.
The Chub is a cautious and shy fish and will only take
the bait slowly after much hesitation. It may be caught
in many different ways — with worms, beetles, or
grasshoppers, but also with dough, breadcrumbs,
or even cherries.
It will very often bite at a trolled spinner.
But without doubt the most enjoyable sport may be had
with an artificial fly. If it is hooked in a fast current on
a fly rod,
the Chub will fight gamely and desperately,
and does not surrender easily

We now leave the fish of prey.
We lay aside the light fly rod,
our spinners and our artificial flies,
for the fish we are turning
to now call for a different
kind of fishing tackle
and a different technique
for catching them

The predominant non-predatory fish
of the lowland waters is the Carp *(Cyprinus carpio)*.
It lives in shoals, in slow-running and
still waters, where there are patches of warmer
water and a rich aquatic flora. The Carp
is a migratory fish, which travels
long distances, especially at night.
The young Carp live in shoals while
the mature fish live in smaller groups,
and it is only when they grow old
that they lead a solitary life

The Carp is an intelligent fish, and not easily hooked.
It is omnivorous, and can be caught with dough, potatoes,
or sweet corn as well as with worms. It calls for
no great skill to land small or medium-sized Carp.
They bite readily, and being inexperienced they are
unaware of the dangers that await them in form of the
angler. A big old Carp, by contrast,
is a crafty master of the art
of survival. It is not
easily hoodwinked, and to catch it
one needs great skill and experience

Large expanses of water, usually reservoirs
in the lowlands, are very popular
with Carp-fishers. The angler can experience
many a dramatic moment, for Carp
in such waters can weigh over forty pounds

To catch such a capital creature is by no means child's
play. First of all we have to convince it that
the bait is real and persuade it to bite. An old
and experienced Carp
which has been on the hook more than once before will
examine the bait thoroughly, and if it notices the tiniest
resistance it will let go of it immediately. But even if it
really bites and we strike at the right moment, it will
fight heroically and long, and its powerful resistance will
subject our tackle to a stern test. It is a long time before
the Carp tires; in its strong body there is an extraordinary
reserve of energy, which the fish uses to the full
in its duel with the angler

rich haul

In Carp-fishing we get to know a completely
new aspect of angling. Peace and quiet
are supreme here, where the angler sits patiently
beside his outstretched rod, waiting
expectantly for the float to dip

The quiet rivers with their dreamy pools
re havens of peace and rest.
rey morning mist, glorious sunsets, a rich catch
nd the restorative peace of Nature, that is
hat lures the angler here

Many relatives of the Carp
live in the lowland waters.
One of these is the Tench *(Tinca tinca)*

Tench tend to prefer the bottom. They feed on maggots,
larvae, and water insects, which they collect
off water plants or pick them up off the bottom.
They prefer still, almost stagnant backwaters,
choked with vegetation; they live in shoals, and reach
a weight of almost ten pounds. We catch them using
ground-bait, generally worms or larvae. The best time for
catching Tench is the early morning or shortly after sunset.
The Tench is no great fighter, and hardly puts up any
resistance at all

One of the most common fish of lowland waters
is the Common Bream *(Abramis brama)*. It is easily
recognized by its narrow body and its highly arched back.
It prefers for its habitat deep parts of the water,
where it lives in shoals, finding its food on the bottom.
It can occasionally reach fifteen pounds in weight
and twenty-eight inches in length, but usually the catch
is not much heavier than two pounds.
Hunting this interesting fish calls for the finest tackle,
for the Bream is very intelligent, shy and cautious,
and a lot of skill is needed to catch a large specimen

The Barbel *(Barbus barbus)* lives only in clean,
fast-flowing waters. We find them chiefly
in the powerful current in the centre
of rivers which have hard and stony beds,
and beneath weirs and locks, although they also
ascend to mountain tributaries on the border
of the trout territory. They live in shoals
near the bottom, and may be caught with
large worms connected to a sinker to keep them
on the bottom. The bite is vigorous and the fish
resists stubbornly after the strike.
To overpower a large Barbel in a strong current
is a real duel and provides exciting sport

We have wandered far along the banks of our rivers
with tackle in hand. Now let us put aside our fishing
tackle, which has been so dear a friend to us, and which
has provided us with so many exciting experiences. Our
subject is still water and the fish that live in it, but no
longer from the point of view of the angler so much as
that of the conservationist

ELPING NATURE

hen fish breed in the natural state there are inevitably
any losses. Some of the reasons for this are unfavourable
eather conditions — for example the drying-out of
awn deposits, or floods that overwhelm the spawn with
ud and sand, as well as countless enemies among other
h, among fish-parasites, among predators of spawn and
ung. But losses such as these have been taken in
count by Nature, and she has provided the fish with
assive reproductive powers to make good the losses.
owever, Nature did not reckon with man, who from
rliest times has sat himself down wherever there was
ater, to plunder the wild-life beneath its surface, at the
me time interfering with the natural surroundings
the fish. The spawning grounds vanished when the
w and level became artificially regulated, the large
ms constructed by man became insurmountable obstacles
migrations upstream, and the cases are not few in
hich man, through irresponsible interference, has managed
destroy all vestiges of water life in many reaches and
any rivers.
oday the angler sits along the banks of a river for its
ace and relaxation. The techniques of angling have
ached such high standards, and the fish have such
sufficient opportunity to reproduce naturally that it is
sential that man should do everything in his power
make good the damage he has done to Nature. Through
tificial breeding and rearing he must try and compensate
ature for all her losses.

The reproductive instinct makes the fish seek out
at the beginning of the spawning season
the most suitable place in the river or in one of its smaller
tributaries, and there they spawn, thus ensuring
the propagation of the species. Some fishes spawn
near their usual habitat while others have to undertake
a long journey upstream, surmounting many obstacles
and strong currents until they reach their spawning grounds.
The trout moves to the spawning grounds.
Again and again it is forced back by the thundering
waters of the weir. But it does not give up,
and repeats its jumps
until finally the obstacle is overcome

Every fish knows instinctively what is the milieu that it
must find in order to provide its spawn with the best
environment for their development.
The Pike spawns in the springtime in the flooded
meadows. The salmon and trout family beat a hole
with their tails in the stony
and sandy bottom of a clear mountain stream, into which
they put their spawn and partly cover the fertilized
eggs with rough sand. In this way the eggs become invisible
among the grains of sand, and escape
the sharp eyes of the predators. Most fish living in
lowland waters spawn in places thickly choked with
weeds, reeds, and other water plants.
The fertilized eggs stick to the plants and so are
comparatively secure from their enemies

Pike, Rainbow Trout and Catfish in their spawning grounds

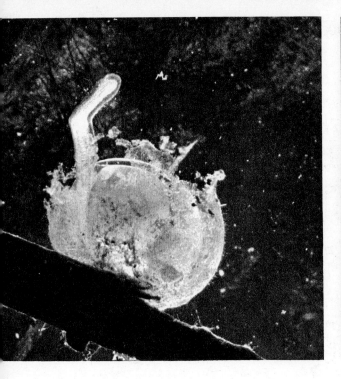

Catfish spawn

The fertilized spawn remains clinging
to the water plants with their sticky surfaces.
As a result of the complicated process
of cell-division, a multitude of cells
comes into being, from which the
individual organs of the future fish develop.
After a time we can clearly distinguish
two eye-points. This marks the stage
shortly before the separation of the spawn.
The swiftness with which the embryos
develop is largely dependent on the
temperature of the water and the
species of fish. Shortly before separation
the skin of the egg comes off and the
new little fish, the fry — frees
itself from its envelope. Slowly the yolk-sac shrinks,
and the baby fish acquires the ability
to feed itself independently. Only a very
small number of the fertilized eggs
survive in nature to the stage of emerging
from the envelope, and only a very small
number of the emergent fry withstand
all threats and dangers with which life
in the water is beset, to grow into adult fish,
themselves capable of reproduction

Ripe spawn of Danubian Salmon

The first necessity for successful artificial breeding
is a sufficient number of healthy spawners, which are
either caught in open water during the spawning season,
or are specially reared in ponds, fish-tanks, or specially
adapted small lakes. The rarer Danubian Salmon are kept
the whole year round in little lakes, where they find
sufficient nourishment and can be easily caught as soon
as the spawning season sets in. Other, less rare fish,
such as Pike-perch, are selected during the autumn
fishing in the larger lakes and kept in smaller pools
or fish-tanks until the spawning season

A Pike caught in a smaller water with a net

Grayling at the spawning grounds

Anglers with an electrical
apparatus engaged
in catching trout

Trout caught with an electrical apparatus

A valuable aid in catching fish
with a view to artificial reproduction
is this electrical apparatus.
The handset generates an electric current,
by means of which the fish
may be caught actually
at their spawning grounds at the moment
of their greatest fecundity

Female Rainbow Trout in spawn

The spawning fish are put into an incubator
and there emptied. The fish is held behind
the anal fin, and the spawn roe
is extracted by means of light stroking
of the belly. The soft roe or milt
is then extracted from a male fish
by the same means, over the hard roe.
The roe and the milt are then well shaken up
and water is poured over them

Pike — female in spawn

The induced spawning of Danubian Salmon
is carried out in exactly the same way
as with other fish, except that
in this case we are dealing
with big, powerful fish some of which
weigh over twenty pounds, so that several
willing hands are necessary

Breeding tanks at the side
of a trout beck

Breeding tanks
for trout arranged
in cascade form

The fertilized eggs are put
into a breeding tank.
They are contained in nets,
through which a constant stream
of fresh water flows.
The size and construction of the
breeding tanks depend
on the size of the fish
and the amount of the spawn

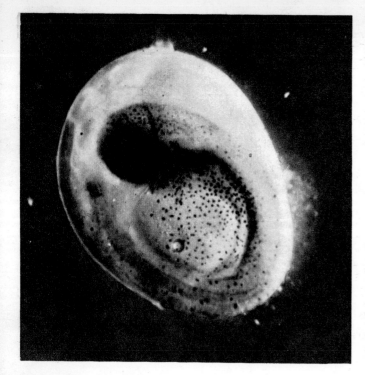

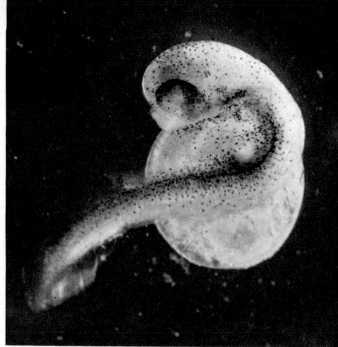

In the later stages
of its development the embryonic Pike
begins to move in the egg,
until it breaks through the elastic
skin of the egg with its tail

Pike fry emerge from the eggs

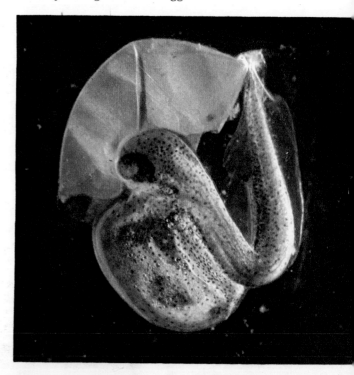

A further series of movements
frees the Pike fry completely
from its envelope

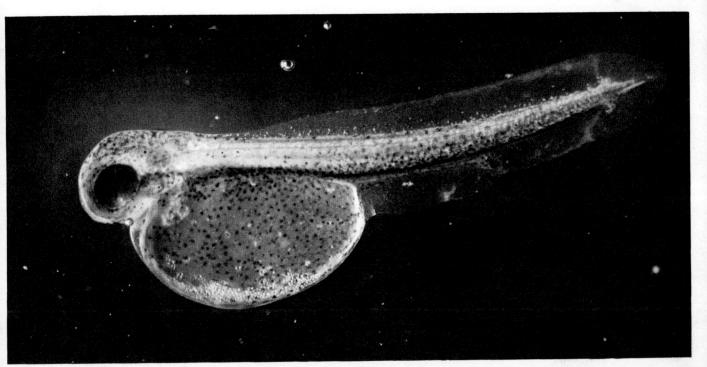

Every species of fish which is capable of being reproduced
artificially presents its own particular requirements for the
extraction of the spawn, and also in the culture
and rearing of the fry,
but in general principle the process is always similar:
the eggs are extracted from the spawning female,
fertilized, and then the spawn is put into various kinds
of incubator or breeding apparatus. After that the young
fry are put into the open water

Millions of young fish of every species
are brought into being every year by
artificial culture. They are either
put straight into natural waters,
or they are kept for a further year
in semi-protected preliminary ponds
and put out as one-year-old fish

In putting out the young Pike fry it is necessary to exercise
great care. The Pike fry must be put into the water
one by one or in small groups along the river bank,
for the Pike is from earliest youth a predatory fish,
and does not spare its own species. If all the fry
are put out in one spot, one fish will devour another
even at the age of three weeks

All the pains which we can take in looking after our waters
will always pay off. The angler knows best the value of this,
who with tackle in hand seeks peace and restorative
solitude beside the water

This was once marshland, a paradise of fish and water birds. Man used to avoid this area, for he feared the bottomless bogs and treacherous swamps, but in the end an abundance of fish lured him here. Since earliest times man has appreciated the tasty meat of fish, and discovered how to obtain it. If the catch was particularly successful, then eventually he would try to ensure for himself access to a continuing supply. Part of a stream would be dammed up, and in the resulting pool the captive fish would be released. In some such way the first fish-tanks may have come into existence, and in this way too the thought may have occurred to man of keeping and breeding fish artificially, in the way familiar to us today.

These giant fish-ponds
arouse wonder and curiosity.
For the most part they were
constructed long, long ago

For centuries these ponds have served for the rearing of
fish. In the smallest ones the fry emerge from the eggs;
in the medium-sized ones the fry are cultivated and
develop and in the larger ones the young fish are
put to grow to marketable size.
Usually the ponds are drained every two years,
and the catch finds its way into the market.
On the appointed day the drainage channels are opened
and the water level sinks slowly. The draining lasts for
up to three days,
and while it continues the fish gather in the deeper part
underneath the dam. The fish are driven towards the centre
from the further parts of the pond with fine nets

In the grey dawn light the fishermen
gather for the first haul

The great nets are drawn across
the fish's kingdom towards the dam

Thousands of Carp and other fish lie struggling in the net

The first fish to be taken out are the more delicate, more easily
damaged ones — the Pike-perch and the Pike — until at last
only the most important fish remains, the Carp

The reward
of long years
of work in the
fish ponds —
handsome
Mirror Carp

The fish are sorted, weighed,
and put into fish-tanks

The fishing-out of a large fish pond is a procedure
which lasts for some days. The first haul is taken at dawn,
and lively excitement reigns by the pond until sunset

In fishing-out a smaller pond, we may
sometimes see fishermen working on into the late
evening by the light of arc lamps

For days on end one netful follows another,
until little by little the pond surrenders
all its inhabitants. The nets become gradually
lighter and lighter, until the last fish
has disappeared and only the muddy bottom
of the pond lies before us

The pond is cleaned out; the discharge channels are closed,
and the water level begins slowly to rise again.
The fishermen gather their equipment together again
and move on to the next pond

The water level has hardly reached its normal
height again, when new inhabitants are put
into the pond and the cycle of life which has
been going on for centuries can begin again

The fishermen have reaped
their 'harvest'
and the pond lies
before us in all
its age-old beauty